Very Funny, Charlie Brown

Selected Cartoons from YOU'RE OUT OF
YOUR MIND, CHARLIE BROWN Vol. 1

Charles M. Schulz

CORONET BOOKS
Hodder Fawcett, London

Reproduced by arrangement with
Fawcett Publications Inc., New York

Coronet edition 1969
Eighth impression 1977

──────────────────────

Printed in Great Britain for
Hodder Fawcett Ltd., Mill Road, Dunton Green,
Sevenoaks, Kent (Editorial Office:
47 Bedford Square, London WC1 3DP) by
C. Nicholls & Company Ltd,
The Philips Park Press, Manchester

ISBN 0 340 10673 5

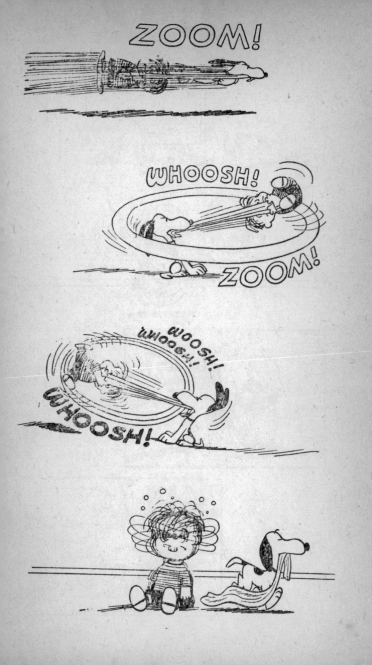

IT'S HAPPENING, CHARLIE BROWN! IT'S HAPPENING JUST LIKE THEY SAID IT WOULD!!
OF COURSE, IT'S HAPPENING.. IT'S SNOWING..WHAT ELSE DID YOU EXPECT THIS TIME OF YEAR?
SNOWING?
GOOD GRIEF..I THOUGHT IT WAS THE FALLOUT!

YOU AND YOUR INSULTS!
BOY, IF YOU WEREN'T A GIRL...
I OUGHTA SLUG YOU A GOOD ONE!
ALL RIGHT, CHARLIE BROWN! COME ON, AND TRY IT!
YOU'RE ALWAYS TALKING BIG! NOW, C'MON! TRY IT!!

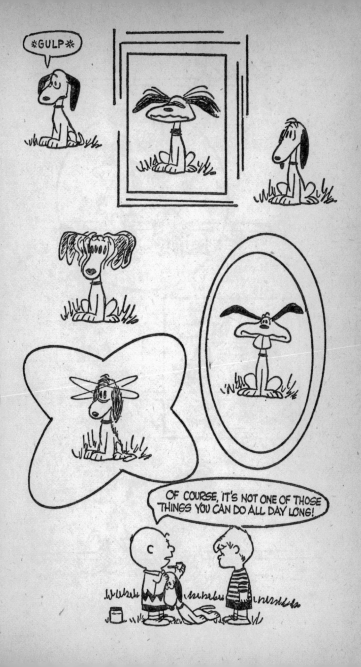

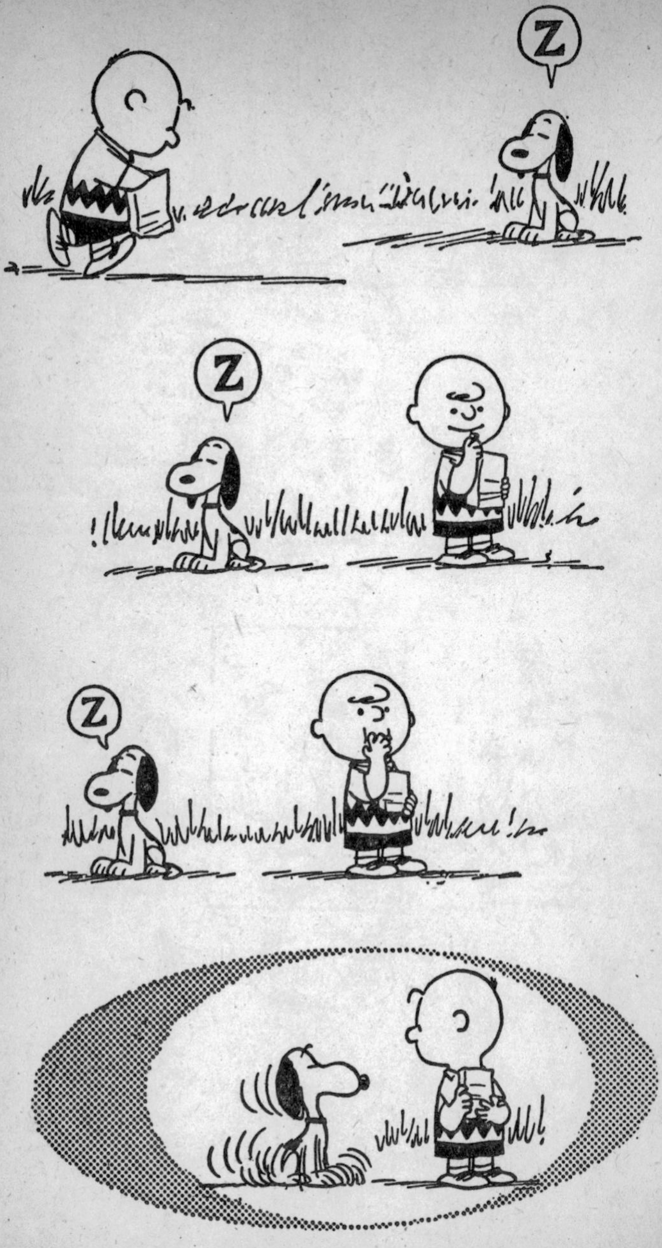
Z
Z
Z

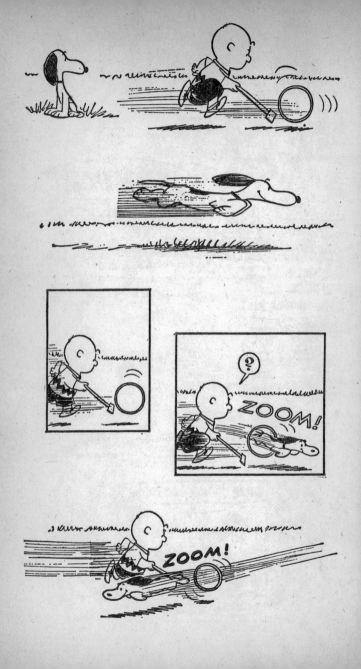

HERE COMES THE FIERCE TIGER SNEAKING UP ON THE HELPLESS CHILD...
SUDDENLY HE POUNCES!

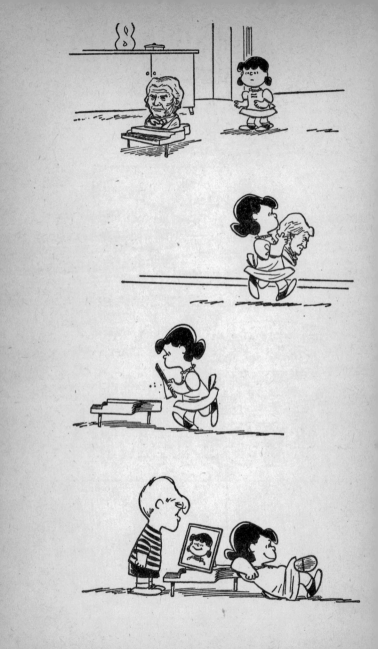

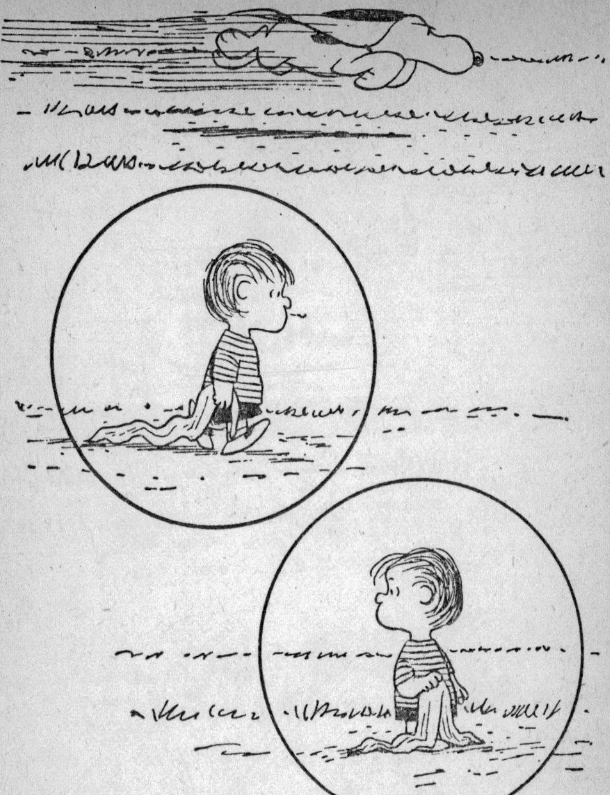

And don't forget about all the other PEANUTS books in CORONET Book editions. Good Grief! More than FIVE MILLION of them in paperback! See the check-list overleaf.

© 1970 United Feature Syndicate, Inc.

Wherever Paperbacks Are Sold

FOR THE LOVE OF PEANUTS

All these books are available at your local bookshop or newsagent, or can be ordered direct from the publisher. Just tick the titles you want and fill in the form below.
Prices and availability subject to change without notice.

CORONET BOOKS, P.O. Box 11, Falmouth, Cornwall.
Please send cheque or postal order, and allow the following for postage and packing:
U.K. – One book 22p plus 10p per copy for each additional book ordered, up to a maximum of 82p.
B.F.P.O. and EIRE – 22p for the first book plus 10p per copy for the next 6 books, thereafter 4p per book.
OTHER OVERSEAS CUSTOMERS – 30p for the first book and 10p per copy for each additional book.

Name ....

Address ....

....